All Night, the Lilies

All Night, the Lilies

Poems by

Caroline Bassett

Cover design by Shay Culligan
Cover image by Klara Kulikova on Unsplash
Author photo by Caroline Bassett

ISBN: 979-8-90146-823-4
Library of Congress Control Number: 2026936260

Kelsay Books
502 South 1040 East, A-119
American Fork, Utah 84003
Kelsaybooks.com

For my children, Lucy and Margot,
and theirs: Beacon, Ela, Silas; Oona

For the furry beloveds too, past and present—
Minga, Sukey, Pippa

Acknowledgments

I thank the following journals where these poems originally appeared, though sometimes in earlier forms.

Naugatuck River Review: "Death of the Matriarch"
Oberon Poetry Magazine: "Love Song for My Daughter"
Of Rust and Glass: "Love in Three Parts"
Quartet Journal: "Halibut Dinner, Dingle, Ireland"
Red Wolf Journal: "Transformation in the Night," "Unbidden they come to me when"

I am also grateful to my teachers over the years:

Thomas R. Smith
Jude Nutter
Deborah Keenan
Gretchen Marquette

Additional thanks to The Loft Literary Center in Minneapolis for supporting writing, poetry, and poets. And to the Literary Witnesses program at Plymouth Congregational Church in Minneapolis for its stellar almost thirty-year sponsorship of visits by remarkable nationally– and locally-known poets and writers such as Donald Hall, Mary Oliver, Gary Snyder, Ted Kooser, and Louise Erdrich.

Many thanks to the members of poetry groups I've been part of for their astute and useful comments: Kathleen Kimball-Baker, Susan Spindler, Steph Brown, Betty Benson, Clover Earl, Shalamar Sibley, Mike Taylor, Paul de Cordova, and Rose Costello.

I'm grateful to my partner Eric Watkins for his patience while I wrote poems.

Contents

Deep in their roots,
all flowers keep the light.

—Theodore Roethke

Daily Bread

How clear, the air today.
See how the sun slants down
          on the new leaves,
          makes them shine.
A pair of cardinals eats together.
The bedsheets will smell sweet tonight
          after drying all day on the line.

A candle flame makes iridescent
the furled petals of the pink tulips—
a sunrise on her dining table.

She notices little crumbs of things
that make a meal,

lets them come to her
in their own time.

*

Three Blue Horses

after Franz Marc

How lovely the large blue horses
that overflow the borders of the painting.

The hills, red behind them, make their coats gleam.

Only then, when you see them, for the first
or fifth or eleventh time, will you wake.

*

When the Wind Came from the North

We didn't need the wind to see
the big Maxwell House Coffee sign
just outside our window—it neoned

red to us just up the Hudson River
from where we lived. We did need
the wind, though, to hear the whistle

signaling shift changes and to bring us
the burnt smell of roasting coffee beans.
Best was the sign with its white cup

tipped up, a drip flashing on and off,
Good to the Last Drop.

✶

Hurricane

From livid clouds rain surges down—
trees sway and snap. The wind,
howling marauder, sends the sound
of cracking trees to us inside
our solid houses.

For a few moments, clouds
pull away to reveal the blue eye
of the sky, the air eerie to breathe,
empty, a ghostly almost-touch
on the skin. A weird total silence

deafens us after the noise. The clouds
move in, the storm returns—
the next morning, five miles from the ocean,
saltwater spray on the house
and two tattered luna moths
by the back door. Why do I still love
the scent of freshly opened trees?

*

Tiger in the Night

In the morning, a birth, nice and quick,
with the usual fuss and mess.
That night the nurse brings me one
of those beings recently forced out

of the dark place of nourishing blood.
It's all wrapped up, this one
labeled *Baby Girl Bassett.*
Lying beside me, she dreams

of that former world—all liquid warmth
with a nearby heart sounding safety
in a steady pulse. If she were a cat, fur still damp,
claws not yet hardened, she would purr.

This swaddled creature sleeps on beside me.
Suddenly, a streak of fierceness shatters
the hospital window, leaps deep into my core.
I am striped, black on orange, sleek and muscled,

now become the true mother of my babe.
And like all mothers, I can be the solace
of soft rain on a parched plain,
but if you touch my child,
I will kill you.

✶

There's No One There to Hear Me

On snowshoes on a perfect winter day—

how blue the sky, like an indigo bunting's back,
how white the snow, like an egret's tufted head,
how bright the sun-wrought sparkles flashing off the snow.

Geese honking above.
No, not gray and brown Canada geese,
Something else.

They make a different sound.
They have
wider wingspreads
longer necks
bigger bodies
black beaks

Swans! I say aloud, in surprise and exaltation
to no one there
to the wilderness around me
to the sky
to the swans themselves,
as if they don't know who they are.

*

Once a Home

Delphiniums grew, blue,
bluer, bluest,
like walking out the back door into the sky.

They lived there for five years,
had a child there,
hung diapers on the line there.

The family moved north,
and years went by.
The house took others in.

When the river flooded,
the people fled;
the house fell.

Not knowing this, the mother
returned to visit
her child's first home.

A slab and a maple
were all that's left.
Moving a rock

from damp ground
leaves its shape below—
absent presence.

*

Choosing Eggs

I look at them carefully,
        each different,

one dusky with tiny freckles,
        one with a smooth light tan,

another dark, speckled with dots,
        or spots at the wide end only.

Each shell color is unique
        but the shape is always egg.

At the co-op I select them one by one,
        loose and free.

I choose each for its own beauty.

✶

Sketches

Red twig dogwoods flush
with rising juice.
We're so glad it's March.

Scallops' tiny blue
metallic eyes,
one in each shell notch,
they never close.
Face-to-face,
what a surprise to mine that blink.

In my kayak
I paddle down the sun-road on the water—
all those sparkles!
What if I just keep going?
Is this what the end is like—
forever brightness?

Little cat, so scared,
hides under the bed.
Bigger cat
watches birds outside the window,
swats her tail and chatters her jaws.
All-grown-up cat,
too many chipmunks in my yard.
Go get 'em!

Nothing's better than lying in bed
with my cat in my arms except—

lying in bed with my cat in my arms,
the windows wide open,
and the summer rain
comes
falling down.

✶

Question for a Horseshoe Crab

Horseshoe crabs are captured and bled by drug companies for their blue, copper-rich blood—useful in detecting bacteria in vaccines for humans.

A species older than dinosaurs,
you still roam the seas. Your body span
larger than a Percheron's hoofprint,
you use your five pairs of legs tipped
with tiny claws to walk the ocean floor.
Ten eyes scattered on your body
find your food. With light receptors
on your pointed tail, you can detect
a full moon, a new moon, even a high tide.
Three hundred million years
and all those eyes—can't you tell us
something about our world?

*

Stillbirth

Galápagos Islands

The Zodiac takes us to a beach where we see
sea lions close up, so unafraid of humans that we stroll
among them. Great dark lumps, they lounge
on the sand sunning themselves, grunting
and turning over. A movement nearby catches
our eyes—a mother has just delivered a stillborn
pup. She nudges it and cuddles it—head, flippers, belly—
and tries to roll it over, now stiff as driftwood.
We shove each other in our eagerness to get back to the boat
away from the dreadful keening—the sea lion
who lifted her head to the sky and wailed.

✶

Idyll and Anti-Idyll

I.

Pull towels and sheets clean
from the machine, put them
into a plastic basket, take it
to the back yard.
Hang them up on a cotton line
with wooden clothespins.
At night, bring it all in,
its scent so heady
it's something
you can hold in your hands.

II.

A simple green cloth bag was all she needed.
My mother put the three kittens in it
and walked down to the pond. Such
a lush place, so warm and humid
with raspberries rampant
and mountain laurel blooming
all June, the pink-white
cups popping pollen when their rims
are touched by, perhaps, passing summer-
brown deer or a copper-colored fox.
Afterwards, when our father brought us home
from playing at the beach, our mother sat
in a chair, a rare sight, her head in her hands.

*

Night-Song

One night, alone at the cabin, wind
slurred through pine branches—a sudden
sound right outside my window.

What is it?
            A birch tree creaking
            as it rubs against another?

No, rougher than that.
            A deer snorting?
            A rabbit screaming, just caught
            by an owl?

No. A large exhaling.
A tear in the veil of night.

            If I fell through that fissure,
            where would I land?
            I might cut through the night
            to tomorrow, already—
            or, go back,
            if back is a place, before time was.

✶

Windows I

Hoboken, New Jersey

I LEAN on my elbows on the enclosed radiator, nice and warm, and look out the big dining room window at the sparkling lights of New York City across the Hudson River. To the north I can see the neon sign of the Maxwell House Coffee plant, a cup tipped onto its side, a last big, fat drop sliding out. That smell of roasting coffee was the smell of snow for me, the wind blowing down the river from the north, and in March the sound of ice floes slamming into each other.

Good
to
the
last
drop

During a tug boat strike, we watch the Queen Mary ocean liner dock herself.

I saw it all from the safe high home of my childhood, the maids' quarters, third floor of a mansion broken into apartments, up the curving servants' staircase, thirty-eight steps. Mother love; father love; siblings squabbling; cats, always cats. My father wore a fedora when he walked to work; my mother decorated snappy hats for herself with found feathers and pieces of lace. My younger brothers and sister got easier jobs around the house—

set the table, put out the milk glasses. The oldest, I got to take out the garbage.

*

"The Little Street in Delft" by Vermeer

In the museum I admire how the painter
made the morning sun look warm
on the bricks of the tall house. In the open doorway
a woman in a white shawl sits mending;
in the alley, a woman in a blue skirt
bends over, sweeping.

I reach my hand into the painting. I touch
the sun-warmed bricks of the house,
hear the scritch of the woman's broom,
smell the dust it has lifted from the ground.

When the woman in the blue skirt turns
to stare at me, I leap backwards,
back into the museum.
I push my way, heart darting
out of my chest, through crowds
looking at Rembrandt's "The Night Watch."

Outside, light sifts
through small spring leaves.
A drop of blood blooms
where the mortar between
the bricks has nicked my palm.

*

Burned-Out House

I had given up sugar.
Yet my brain thought of nothing
            but candies, cakes, and cookies,
            of mascarpone, of macadamias bathed in golden honey,
            of ice cream, of puddings—rice, bread, chocolate,
            of candied things—ginger, pecans, walnuts.

Sugar-deprived, my soul turned sour.
I scowled. I shouted. I honked my horn—
at mothers pushing strollers, at the limping
injured squirrel in the street, at the chained
barking dog who lived two houses down.
But even without sugar, my yammering mind
went quiet, passing the silent, burned-out house
where a man had recently died.

*

"The Adoration of the Magi" and Sandro Botticelli's Self-Portrait

He turned away from the scene of adoration
he'd just completed.

He'd painted his patrons,
the Medicis, as the Three Kings.
In a red tunic, Cosimo's son Lorenzo
struts, signaling
his Magnificent status to come.

Botticelli portrayed himself, his sideways
sharp gaze peering out of the painting, not
to doubt his faith or scorn the Medicis
or for boredom with his craft—
instead, he wanted to know

how a man with too much sight
can live in this world.

*

Switchboard

Dazed after the half-day's training, I dawdled
for a while, walking through Washington Square Park
in Greenwich Village, before heading north
to Union Square, to the publishing house
where I worked one summer in college.

The lights in the panel in front of me kept blaring,
the sockets yelling to be filled by the right plug,
the voices in the headset demanding connection.

Lights flashed: *Outside line, please.*
Flash: *I asked for Bob Giroux, not the mailroom. Connect me!*
Flash: *Where's Bruce? Has he gone out for lunch yet?*

As the day went by, it got harder and harder
to pay attention, keep track. I worked alone
in the small office, and the calls kept coming.
Did Roger Straus want an outside line?
When is old Mr. Farrar coming in?
I was glad that I wasn't the one who dropped
that call to London.

All these years later, after a scolding sister
who rebuked me for every email not acknowledged,
after lovers I no longer charmed
and who turned to the beds of others,
after friends at odds, I know a lot now
        about plugs put in the wrong holes,
        crossed communication,
        broken lines.

*

Solace for Russ

He attends our reunion three days after
the death of his wife. We're all friends of fifty years—
solid bonds in the Peace Corps listening
to Moroccan rhythms and eating fava bean tagines.
His wife had been sick a long time. He'd tended
her for months. No family left. Here, release
of a kind before he returns to the empty house.
Conversations and laughter—we visit museums
and Fort Sumter, eat shrimp homestyle.

Russ is not a ghost, just quiet. We talk about Morocco,
remember playing Arabic rummy for hours in the sunshine,
riding my Vélosolex motorbike to pick up hash
cookies, going to American movies dubbed in French—
except Elvis's songs. Together we become
a hammock for him, grasping it on all sides,
rocking him lightly so he knows we're there.
He lets himself rest, supported, and relinquishes
the fight to be other than bereaved.

*

On the Bus Home from Fès to Casablanca

I know enough to sit on the shady side
and toward the front because the rear bounces
way too much on the rough roads. A Moroccan woman
in a tattered djellaba sits beside me. We greet each other
in Arabic. Soon she leans against me. With my American
boundaries, I move away. She tilts her body onto mine
and again I try to keep my space, though on a bus
there's not much room. She continues to tip towards me.
Finally, I know what to do. I move my lumpy bag
with snacks and a water bottle onto the floor
and let my body rest against hers. We both fall asleep.

*

Magnum Mysterium

The catwalk, a narrow shelf sixteen inches wide,
gave us kids a slender opportunity
to sidle along and climb up onto the roof.
Don't look down, we told ourselves.
Three stories—too far to fall,
to even think of falling.
And I thought—if I did fall,
being a featherless creature, I couldn't
fly and swoop up and away.

And if I did fall, who would weep?
My brother, the one who turned against me—
would the live coal of sorrow
burn compassion into his heart's
hard core? With more sunlight from our parents,
would my cranky sister become
a whole sweet fruit? Would my parents
turn to drink even sooner?
Or later? Or not at all?

O magnum mysterium.

*

Chiaroscuro

Today, on the silver lake, ribbons of ebony appear
made from ripples by the wind. From underwater,
something gathers itself, lifts itself to the surface,
and becomes three-dimensional, a black and white

razor-beaked loon. Eagles fly overhead creating
turbulence in the air. A feather falls and floats
on the water. Around the point into a bay,
a commotion in the water—a creature emerges,

runs along the shore and disappears behind a bush—
an otter carrying a crayfish in its mouth.
On shore, a turtle lays her eggs,
pushing them into the nest she has made

in the sand. Near her there's a marauded one
with rubbery white shells strewn
all about. Her work done, the turtle slips
silently into the water. She leaves no evidence

that she was ever there. The lucid blue sky
arches overhead until darkening cumulus clouds
gather foretelling rain.
rain•sun•death•snow•sun•rain•life•snow•death•sun

*

Late November: A Portrait

Dingy rains fill up cavities.
Sharp frosts deepen cracks.
An abandoned fountain in the garden
    lies on its side, split open.
Gray, flat, pewter—silver with no shine.
Ashen, sooty, thick—smoke with no fire.
Leaden, heavy, dreary—clouds dense with no purpose.

Some days morning sunshine gilds
    tree trunks and branches—
    their furrowed columns and girders
    glow with brief warmth.

Damp is cold, cold is damp.
    Dead fish live inside your shirt, next to your skin.
    November.

Dried wildflower stalks
    rattle in the wind.
Underground,
    life rests,
    dark and protected.

Sleet, mournful as bagpipes,
    presses sodden leaves
    onto frozen ground.

The sullen sky makes the sun feel useless.

Instead, attention shifts from
the big fire in the sky
to the smaller ones
burning in the hearth.

✶

Halibut Dinner, Dingle, Ireland

A slab of white fish floating
on a pink sea of red pepper sauce,
cushioned on clouds of mashed potatoes,
crossed with spears of asparagus. No bones
to catch in the throat.

In this land encircled by sea,
the long beauty of churches and forts
stand after one thousand years.
An oratory of flat gray stones,

a door to the west, a window
to the east looks out upon
a rising sun, hope against
a bleak, torn, ragged life,

memories of babes who slid out
and died soon, unbaptized,
doomed to Limbo, buried
at night, a stone for a pillow,

in the flinty unconsecrated ground.
For a mother who knows her child
will never see God—what a catch
in the throat.

✶

Circuits

The polar bear at the Como Zoo
circles her pool and circles some more.

Her white hulk takes a breath,
dives underwater,

touches a post with her left paw,
swims behind a fake rock put there

to fool her. She pushes off
against it with her right paw,

surfaces. As I watch the bear,
I fear the future of all beings

captive in cages
of steel or gold or air.

*

Raven

Down from the sky,
black lightning.

Rare this far south,
even more so in the city,
twice the size of a crow,
it lands,

too large
for the world
of the birdbath,
almost toppling it.

It dips in its stout beak
and carries out
a piece of sky.

Cracked open, the robin's eggshell
leaves behind, stuck to it,
flesh, a feather, a foot.

Will I weep for the dead fledgling?
Or rejoice that it has fed
the raven's young

as the terrible grace
of those black wings
heads north and
leaves me behind.

*

"The Duke and Duchess of Urbino"

Piero della Francesca, ca. 1473

We see his profile as he gazes
at his wife. Typical Renaissance
scenery behind them, a river

and farmland in the foreground,
mountains bluing into the distance.
She is pale against his robust coloring

and red cloak. Pale according
to the esthetics of the time, blond hair
in intricate headdress, black velvet gown,

jewel-studded collar, she looks
toward him—his strong brow,
one intense eye, the other lost

in a tournament, the bridge of his nose
removed by surgeons to give him
better vision, protection from assassins.

The remaining eye had made many things,
a grand library and scribes in his scriptorium,
a humanistic court held in his Ducal Palace.

A lack of cruelty in his gaze. Instead, love
for his wife, Battista Sforza, who at twenty-five,
died giving birth to their seventh child.

Of her, he said, *she was the delight*
of my public and private hours.
No emotion shows in this formal portrait,

but the scenery behind them
connects them.

*

Windows II

592 ½ North Street, Vermont

WE leave the kitchen window open to the Vermont winter so the cat can get in. Landlady scolds us for letting the heat out. Much love in our three-quarter-sized bed—he is six feet three inches, tries to sleep diagonally. I say that I cut myself in two each night, one half of me on either side of him.

A waif he's trying to save calls on the phone. I am wife and that's that, but he gives her his sister's new bike.

Where
is
he?

On cold nights I watch through the narrow bedroom window for my husband to return. Where is he?

Why is he so late? The medical student says, *I was studying.* The first leaves of doubt and mistrust sprout on the tree.

✶

Windows III

608 Eastmoor Drive, Iowa

WHEN I go out the back door, I step into the sky, a stand of delphinium. Loud and rowdy volleyball parties out there with the other medical interns and residents and their wives. Brats and beer; plenty of beer.

Later, I'm looking out

black soil of Iowa grows
yellow corn and blue
delphinium

the small window in the shower behind the curtain—outside at the Iowa summer night whose hot weight I feel. I am pregnant. When he finally gets home, my husband looks for me all over the house, alarmed, then contrite and loving when he finds where I've been hiding.

In January he's the one doing the searching again—so unusual. Mostly it was me looking for him to come back. Now he's waiting by the front door, hoping for my return with our new baby. I left, couldn't find a motel, needed to nurse, came back. He sticks around for a while.

Many years later I go back to see the house, but it isn't there anymore. A flood swept it away, leaving only the foundation and a maple tree I planted in the front yard.

✶

Windows IV

1264 New Scotland Road, New York

TO the west coast where his job didn't work out. To New York State, where it did. But I hated Albany. Old in a worn-out way, not gracious or stately. No pride of place. Dreary winters and not enough snow. I try to take photos of ugliness but find it hard to do.

Walking down the street there, my only friend looks in a café window and sees him holding hands with Judy Merrill. Confrontation. After a while, reconciliation, but without acknowledgment of my unhappiness. A fire scorches the bark off of one side of the tree.

Why don't I?

I don't let my children
see me weeping. Why don't I?
It's not the kind of sorrow
they should know.

*

Death of the Matriarch

A hot day. Sucking lemon drops I wander concrete paths
of the National Zoo. I'm looking for those so like us
and so not—their hands are hands,
their feet like hands. They nap after lunch.
But the Gorilla House has closed, and a gray van

is backed up close to the loading dock. As I wait outside,
I chat with Pierre in French because I've overheard him
speaking his own language with another zookeeper.
He's agitated and uneasy and keeps looking around,
especially at the van. Then, because no passersby

will understand us, he tells me a secret—
that's what he calls it, a *secret*—
Les vétérinaires ont euthanazié la martiarche.
At that moment, there is activity at the back door.
Barely visible to onlookers, a stretcher with something

lumpy covered in cloth is loaded on.
Pierre crosses himself reverently, openly
wipes away tears. And then, like the biblical
wailing at my cousin Laura's funeral two years ago,
the gorillas, abandoned in the building,

begin to roar and thump and bang.
Years later, on sultry days when I unwrap
a lemon drop, I remember Pierre's stricken face
and his tears for his *grande dame,* so like us and so not—
her hands were hands, her feet like hands.

✶

A Medieval Musician-Angel, Along with Seventeen Others, Blows His Horn in the 11th-Century Crypt of the Bayeux Cathedral

Painted in fresco on a dark
ochre background, where the tops
of the pillars flare out
into the ceiling,
he's blowing his *chalémie.*

Gathered at the waist by a rope,
his monk's robe brushes the floor.
His powerful wings
arch out, protecting him
from the shadows gathered behind him.
A simple halo glows golden.

Brother monk, are you praying to God?
Are you asking, along with Handel in his *Messiah*
using the resonant words of Isaiah,
that warfare be done with,
that iniquity be vanquished,
that we may live together as one people?

You seek comfort with your music.
Though your Lord may not
be ours,
your harmonies give us
solace—and we
need it now, yes, to prevail
we need it
now.

*

The Great Dying

The "Great Dying," a mass extinction, marked the end of the Permian era about 250 million years ago and killed most marine life due to global warming.

Trilobites' lobed bodies
become stone flowers,
    lie piled and jammed together
    on the sunny fossil bed.
People step all over them, now that they are rock.

Five hundred million years ago, trilobite,
ammonite, brachiopod,
    lived together
    in the cool dark depths
of the great coral sea that became the Ohio River.

Trilobites, ammonites, brachiopods
moved about on the bottom there,
    then perished, all.
    Turned solid and choiceless,
they endure now in the blasting light,

on the burning surface, of the sunny
fossil bed. And what of us—
    more than seven billion of us?
    What will remain when our turn comes?

Of our soft flesh, nothing.
Of our harder hollow bones? A chip.
Of our teeth? A fragment.
Trilobite, ammonite, brachiopod—
Mes semblables, mes frères.

*

Unbidden they come to me when

they will, late or soon. I don't, I can't invite them.
It's up to them when they visit.
Months after my parents' deaths,

they appeared as a pair of wintering loons
in gray plumage on a gray sheet
of ocean. Always together, they swam

perilously distant from the rest of the flock.
They knew I had seen them.
On a soft fall evening, a doe, my aunt,

separated herself from the herd. Alone,
she stepped out into the middle
of the field and looked at me calmly,

greeted me with a flick of her ears,
then turned to rejoin the others.
I could feel the sadness in the squirrel's eyes,

as motionless, it stared at me
through my study window. It spoke to me
as my cat, sorry she had died too soon.

I don't know why these visits
happen to me. It feels like a special gift,
a chance for a moment to be again

with ones my heart clings to.
The visits come from a realm
that I don't believe in.

But I believe the visits.

*

Rain Bird

after Rumi

The rain bird longs for rain.
She can drink only rain,
though the many blue-
and-white-tiled fountains
in her city flow day and night
with fresh water. Dry-
tongued, she stares
at the blank-eyed sun.

Elsewhere, the hyacinth longs
to bloom, but the earth grips
her bulb in its frozen fist.

And I long for my beloved
home, north of here and west,
with many lakes and sweet, clear air.

The rainbird, the hyacinth, and I,
no way to alter our fates for now.

✶

falling through the universe

i don't know
where i am
what anything is
where anything is, flailing
as i fall, nothing
to latch on to, no way
to orient myself—slipping
through space, i reach
for words
delectable or disgusting,
for metaphors that will amaze
a heart, for closure
with all the right colors.
i'm seeking the sacred
in the midst of the mundane—
saddlebags of hyssop pollen
on a honeybee's legs, a mother
cat nursing her five all-black kittens,
rain giving water to the dry earth.

when i finally touch
ground, who
will i be?

✶

Windows V

Loring Pasta Bar, Dinkytown, Minnesota

TANGO music is syncopated, sexy, sultry. Sad, minor key. Songs about lost loves. Missing the company of men in my increasingly failed marriage, I find a way to be touched, but safely.

I get dressed up, even for weekly classes in Dan's apartment with big mirrors on one wall and smooth oak wood floors. We pair up and rotate partners. We get into the close embrace, the essential tango position, an upside-down V with pelvis and legs separated, heads close, chests together. *You get used to those bumps,* says Dan to the male dancers.

Learn to follow.

The man leads, you follow. It's all silent—he shifts his weight—forward or back, side to side, rotates his shoulder a fraction, changes where his hand is on your back, and you read it and react—in that same instant.

It works best if you can put yourself into a tango trance. It's like putting on a winter cap and pulling it most of the way down over your eyes. Close yourself off from the world. Focus your whole attention on what his body bids you do. Turn yourself off. Be receptive. Be passive, except for a few beats when he must wait for you to execute some ornamental steps as you swing your feet in patterns on the floor or slide your leg up his.

I take years of lessons and classes. I go to milongas—tango dances. I buy a new red dress and matching shoes. I put on makeup and expensive perfume. I stand off to the side, indicating that I'm available to dance. But I rarely get danced. I'm too old. Whatever age I am, I am older than I should be.

> *So much depends upon*
> *being asked*
> *to dance.*

One night I turn my back on the scene and instead stare out the window at neon lights in the rainy street. There's more solace for my loneliness there than in all the people behind me. But I do love the music.

*

"Old Man and His Grandson"

Domenico Ghirlandaio, ca. 1490

In the boy's face, the old man sees
himself as he once was,
innocent of the workings

of the world. He wears a red robe
and gazes down at his grandson,
six years old, blond curls, red doublet

and cap, his delicate hand
laid on his grandfather's chest.
The boy looks up

into the old man's face
with awe and wonder, that this great
one is giving him his full attention.

He ignores his grandfather's bulbous nose,
deformed with warts, as love flows
up from the boy's hand

into the old man's heart.
From him, sympathy streams down
to his grandson. He knows

it will be impossible to prevent iniquity
from insinuating itself into the Garden
that is this sweet boy.

*

Love in Three Parts

At bedtime, my two-year old grandson, Beacon, watches a Czech cartoon about a mole, Krtek, and his pal, Mouse. Beacon falls in love with Mouse. He misses Mouse when he is out of sight. He wants to see Mouse; he wants Mouse to be with him. During the day he asks when he can see Mouse again.

In Paris a few summers ago, my brother, Tom, who was working in the Netherlands, took the train and visited me for the weekend. We walked for seven miles. From the Eiffel Tower we crossed the Seine, sauntered down the Champs-Elysées, strolled past the Louvre to Notre Dame, and ended at the Place de la Bastille in the midst of a rowdy Gay Pride celebration, resplendent with rainbows. It had become his city.

Love begins. I saw it.

I was with my daughter, her husband, their son, and their newborn. Ten whole days with my child mothering her own baby daughter. We talked of daily things and laughed the way we do. Nothing was different: speech did not slow, pauses did not lengthen, touches did not get tenderer, the air did not shimmer and sing. And yet, it felt this way. As the waves come onto the shore and seep into the sand, that other world flowed into this one, alive as light.

Love continues. I felt it.

He pressed a pillow down on my love and suffocated it, did my former husband.

Beacon will outgrow his love for Mouse. But not Tom's for Paris.

Love enters, it lives. Love leaves. I know it.
I write these things. I do not understand them.

✶

The Tide Turns at the Breachway

While you're standing around on the beach, remember
that the waves will come up and get your towels wet.
Hours later, long after you've finished your picnic, you'll see
that the ocean's water has been withdrawing, revealing
quahogs and mussel shells for your children
to gather. From where you are, you can't notice
the moment the tide turned—it's imperceptible.

So when you come to see me in Rhode Island,
let's be sure to visit the Charlestown Breachway
which opens the brackish Ninigret Pond to the ocean.
In that narrow inlet, lined with pink and gray
boulders, you can see for yourself, in front of your eyes,
what is otherwise unnoticeable—
the changing tide. The water coming in
thrusts aside strands of seaweed, collides
with the pond water being pulled out.
For a moment they clash, then flow together
in the direction appointed by the moon.

When I see you, let's write love songs
for the Breachway, and to the ocean,
whose great heart beats ceaselessly
for the whole world.

*

Love Song for My Daughter

Midway through her song cycle performance
she tells the audience about her kidney disease,
about empty cysts filling up the space
where tissue should be.

Her disease is like losing an eye—
once gone, gone forever.
Her new medication
makes her constantly thirsty,
a different, deeper, kind of thirst
from yours and mine—unslakable.

She speaks to us about how she welcomes
her thirst—it's her muse, insisting that she write
and keep singing. She's reached beyond dread,
she says, and has found solace in a line of Rumi:
Do not seek for water. Be thirsty.

*

Earthen Oyster

Don't forget what the gardener
knows—dried wildflower stalks

rattle in wind,
frost hardens soil,

sleet from a sullen sky
presses sodden leaves

onto frozen ground,
where

seeds rest
roots sleep

until the hungry sun
eats ice from mulch

and a trowel pries open
the earthen oyster

to find the loamy
womb

from which all life
springs.

*

A Blameless House

To drive past the house you lived in for many years
long ago, is, of course, to find it blameless.

You left the house, two in from the corner,
after you lost your job. The sorrow

lies in you, doesn't it? Why put iron bands
around its foundation to hold in your weeping,

not around you? Its cottage garden
is now weeds. Even they struggle

under the neighbor's huge maple. The yard
is now tightly fenced, a garage added in back.

Behind it, in a neglected corner,
bindweed and deadly nightshade grow.

To return to the house you lived in—
        years of children and piano lessons
        cats, purring or sick,
        packing the car in the driveway for trips to see grandparents
        birthday parties with candles and cake—

is to find it standing still and square, tan and bland,
as it always was. But since your sadness lingers and lives on

there, do this: gather it up and move it
into your heart. Find a spacious place to plant
your worthy grief, and lilacs

*

Rain Fell. I Felt a Little Happiness.

from Zagajewski, a line from "Café"

The rain fell on dry earth. We held
each other's hands and ran out into it,
opening our mouths to receive it,
as music amplifies souls,
as bread fills bellies,
as words cloak us
in gray armor or red velvet robes
for dancing.

✶

He Comes to Me

He comes to me in a field of daises
but I don't see him.
I am beguiled by the tangy flower
scent, and all those yellow suns
encircled by a breath of white cloud.

He comes to me in a field of snow
but I don't see him.
I'm having too much fun
sliding by on skis, poling fast
down a sparkling hill.

He comes to me in a field of parquet,
but I don't see him.
I'm making squash soup for supper,
slicing the onions first.

He comes for me in a field of white sheets
and blinking machines,
and I, finally, lie down.

✶

Windows VI

New Windows

THE OLD windows
tipped open only
a sliver in winter,
letting in tiny slices
of cold air,
not enough to deepen sleep.

The new windows, a new design,
wind wide all the way—
slick as silk,
soft as soap,
smooth as an owl's swoop.

Now they let in the sweet air.
Now I can hear the silent stars
slide by all night long
until the din of dawn hushes them—
birds dogs babies
singing barking crying

They usher in scents as winter ends—
the regal purple lilacs' sudden flood of smell
that opens the door to the first day of spring,
flush plush pink roses—
so redolent that they fill the breeze,
my bright moon-splashed Casablanca lily,
spicy-fragrant as a jar of cloves,
stella maris, in my garden's sea of green.

O my lovely new windows,
you have opened up
the vault of the firmament
to me.
I step out into it.

✶

Elegy for My Old Lady Cat

Some, says Milosz, place millet or poppy seeds
on graves to feed the dead
who return disguised as birds.

On yours, I put a conch shell
because I like it,
though it has nothing to do with you.

You have never been to the sea,
and you wouldn't like it—
the foot-high waves bigger than you.

I've covered your space with autumn leaves
because bare soil is anathema
to a gardener.

There's a marker
with your dates,
and I put down

moonstones from the beach
that shine in the dark
as your eyes did

when you blinked them barely open
at night
when I got home late.

*

I Have Held the Summer Dawn in My Arms

after Rimbaud

Reluctant to leave the night,
the waning moon sets with a sigh.

All night the lilies promiscuously fling
their perfume throughout the garden.

Dawn opens with bird song.
Some sweet—liquid notes of the wood thrush,
a single silver thread of water falling over rocks.
Others harsh like the oven bird's,
"teacha teacha teacha," the dread
of being shut up in the school room.

I have held the summer dawn in my arms
and I have bloomed like flowers awakened
to the rising of the light.

✶

Notes

"Her Daily Bread" is dedicated to my friend Joan who got through the Covid pandemic in this way.

"Three Blue Horses" is a painting by Franz Marc in the Walker Art Center in Minneapolis, Minnesota.

"Solace for Russ" is dedicated to my Peace Corps friend RC.

"The Great Dying." "*Mon semblable, mon frère*" (my familiar, my brother) from Baudelaire's *Les Fleurs du Mal.*

The building referred to in "Halibut Dinner, Dingle, Ireland" is the Gallarus Oratory in Dingle.

About the Author

Long before her recent 80th birthday, Caroline Bassett transplanted herself from Hoboken, New Jersey, to Minneapolis, Minnesota, where she lives happily writing poetry and gardening during the growing season. Even before that relocation, she served in the Peace Corps in Casablanca, Morocco, for two years where she taught English as a Foreign Language. Her poems, one of which was nominated for a Pushcart Prize, have appeared in several journals. In 2021, she was chosen for and completed the Loft Literary Center's Year-Long Writing Project in Poetry. Five years ago, she organized "Good Hearts," a book group that reads a poetry collection every other month. Carrie also chairs Literary Witnesses, an almost thirty-year old public poetry series sponsored by a prominent church.

www.ingramcontent.com/pod-product-compliance
Lightning Source LLC
LaVergne TN
LVHW010630100826
845148LV00014B/3180
* 9 7 9 8 9 0 1 4 6 8 2 3 4 *